portrait of PALM SPRINGS

FARCOUNTRY PRESS

PHOTOGRAPHY BY **TOM BREWSTER** • FOREWORD BY **JAMES W. CORNETT**

ISBN 10: 1-56037-470-5
ISBN 13: 978-1-56037-470-1

© 2007 by Farcountry Press
Photography © 2007 by Tom Brewster

For more information about our books, write Farcountry Press, P.O. Box 5630, Helena, MT 59604; call (800) 821-3874; or visit www.farcountrypress.com.

Created, produced, and designed in the United States.
Printed in China.

12   11   10   09   08   07   1   2   3   4   5   6

Above: Sunrise brightens the summit of Mount San Jacinto, seen from the Mesquite Golf and Country Club's golf course.

Title page: The outskirts of Palm Springs erupt with color after spring rains, when verbena carpets the valley in bright fuchsia.

Front cover: Native fan palms thrive in Indian Canyons, above a field of brittlebush flowers in full bloom.

Back cover: Towering palm trees are silhouetted by a pastel sky in Palm Springs.

3

Sunrise provides a colorful backdrop to the striking silhouettes of two palm trees.

FOREWORD

James W. Cornett

One hundred miles east of Los Angeles, beyond the mountains that dominate the Southern California skyline, is a desert valley made famous not by its spectacular scenery but by the people who live and vacation there. Billionaire Bill Gates has a home in the valley, as does writer Joseph Wambaugh. The late and great comedian Bob Hope was perhaps the most famous resident if you don't count Frank Sinatra, William Powell, or Arnold Palmer. Countless presidents have vacationed in this desert oasis, and President Dwight Eisenhower and President Gerald Ford built homes here.

The valley of which I am speaking is the Coachella Valley, better known as the place where the city of Palm Springs was incorporated in 1938. Today, there are nine incorporated cities in the valley, and two, Indio and Palm Desert, have grown into the region's largest municipalities.

The origin of the name "Coachella" is obscure. My money is on the tale that claims it to be a bastardization of the Spanish word *conchita,* meaning "little shell." Walking through the desert in and around the cities of La Quinta and Coachella reveals the basis of the story. Everywhere, on top of the sand, are tiny shells of underwater creatures that lived in the waters of an ancient lake that covered much of the region just a few hundred years ago. The ancient lake is gone, replaced by the Salton Sea, California's largest body of water.

Though celebrity-watching is a popular pastime for residents and visitors, most people come to the Coachella Valley today to experience the outdoors. The Coachella Valley is a northwestern extension of the Colorado Desert, with the Colorado River as its eastern boundary. This subdivision of the much larger Sonoran Desert is second only to Death Valley as the hottest and driest region in North America. In this climate, the sun shines almost every day and, because of the area's low elevation (below sea level in the valley's southeastern end), temperatures during the winter months are in the 70s, even in January. The chances that a given day will be sunny are so high that I advise everyone to plan their social activities as though it will never rain again!

Although golf and tennis are popular with many residents and visitors, spurred by television coverage of tournaments, I have always been partial to the region's wilderness. The natural environments that lie within and surround the Coachella Valley are so special that more private and government agencies have spent more time and money to protect wilderness in this region than in any other comparably sized region in the country.

The protected areas, most of which are open to the public, read like pages from a wonders of the modern world book. Mount San Jacinto State Park, which protects the slopes of Mount San Jacinto, the steepest peak in North America, can be visited by riding up the Palm Springs Aerial Tramway. The Indian Canyons Tribal Park, managed by the Agua Caliente Band of Cahuilla Indians, contains Palm Canyon, the largest natural desert palm oasis on the planet. Joshua Tree National Park forms the northern boundary of the valley and is the only park in the Southwest that contains two completely different deserts, the Mojave and Sonoran. The Salton Sea State Recreation Area protects much of the shoreline of its namesake, the Salton Sea—California's largest lake and one of the best bird-watching places in America.

If diversity inspires you, take a drive up Highway 74 through the heart of the Santa Rosa and San Jacinto Mountains National Monument. In less than an hour you'll experience a half-dozen plant communities, which is why the roadway is locally known as the Palms to Pines Highway. Enjoy a walk across the infamous San Andreas Fault and into a lush palm oasis at the Coachella Valley Preserve.

Whether it's celebrity-watching or bird-watching, the valley is, first and foremost, a visual experience. There is much to feed the eyes and most of this visual feast basks in bright sunshine. For this reason, the valley has attracted fine artists for more than a century, starting with the painter Carl Eytel and the photographer Stephen Willard in the early part of the twentieth century.

As a photographer of sorts myself, I have paid particular attention to image makers and have become familiar with the talents of many photographers—some of whom have passed on, some of whom have moved on, and some of whom have stayed. One who has stayed is Tom Brewster, and he has been photographing the valley's scenes in all their splendid diversity for nearly thirty years. Whereas the overwhelming majority of fine art photographers specialize in one type of subject, Tom has had the luxury of being able to capture images of just about every aspect of Coachella Valley life. He has been here for so long, in so many arenas, and with so fine an eye, that I can think of no other photographer whose work merits a photographic exposé of the Coachella Valley in all of its forms. I hope you enjoy this visual experience.

James W. Cornett is a desert ecologist and writer who has lived in Palm Springs and the Coachella Valley since 1972. For nearly thirty years he was at the Palm Springs Desert Museum, retiring in 2005 as its Director of Natural Sciences. His most recent book is *Wonders of the Coachella Valley.*

The giant rectangular granitic blocks in Joshua Tree National Park seem to cradle the last glimmer of moonlight before it sets. You might spot a lizard in one of the cracks. The reptiles found in the national park include one tortoise, eighteen species of lizards, and twenty-five varieties of snakes.

Right: The mouth of Andreas Canyon is shady, even in the heat of summer. More than 150 species of plants grow in a half-mile radius of the oasis.

Below: Perennial streams, such as the wildflower-lined Chino Creek, enrich the desert ecosystem by providing life-giving moisture to plants and animals.

6

Facing page: Joshua trees are the dominant large vegetation in the high desert near Palm Springs. The upstretched limbs reminded early Mormon settlers of the Biblical story of Joshua reaching his arms to God.

Below, left and right: Mojave mound cactus is a prolific bloomer that favors rocky slopes. It grows from 6 to 12 inches tall and produces red fruits after blooming.

Above, left and right: Dancers at a powwow don colorful, elaborate clothing and ornaments for competitions. There are twenty-five American Indian bands and tribes in Southern California.

Right: The Coachella Valley Preserve protects several desert dune fields and palm oases in the approximately 20,000 acres of fragile lands fed by springs rising along several faults. These desert fan palms shelter birds and lizards under the layers of hanging fronds. The rare western yellow bat is known to roost here.

Left: A dusting of snow on Mount San Jacinto, which towers above Tahquitz Creek Golf Resort, demonstrates just how much cooler it is on the slopes, high above the valley floor.

Far left: The Rancho La Quinta Golf Resort has two 18-hole golf courses. The name Tahquitz is given to several natural features in Southern California. Luiseño Indian legend says that a spirit-demon named Tahquitz was partial to collecting the souls of people, particularly beautiful maidens.

These pages: The wide-open Devil's Garden just north of Palm Springs provides a clear view of Mount San Jacinto. The lowlands were so named because of the six species of cacti that reach impressive densities there.

Right: Brittlebush brightens the entrance to Chino Canyon.

Far right: The Palm Springs International Airport serves more than one million passengers a year. Fourteen airlines provide more than fifty daily departures.

Right: The Palm Springs Convention Center was expanded in 2006 and calls itself "The Meeting Oasis."

Below: The Moorten Botanical Gardens shelters thousands of examples of desert cacti and plants, grouped by geographic region. Many are extremely rare species from desert environments around the world. This prickly pear blossom and fruit occur in the region.

These pages: The Thousand Palms Oasis was long a water source for the Cahuilla Indians and other travelers. In 1877 the Desert Land Act allowed white settlers to claim some oasis land as homesteads. Today the fragile area, which includes sand dunes, is preserved in the Coachella Valley Preserve.

These pages: Distinctively down-curved bills identify the flocks of curlews wintering on the Salton Sea. Close to half of the total bird species known to exist in the United States have been documented at the Salton Sea—2 to 3 million birds a day in the winter. The sea's increasing salinity, however, does not bode well for the future of the fish and aquatic life and, thus, the future of the birds that feed upon them.

Above: Brittle bush flowers and cholla and barrel cacti thrive in the arid environment of Devil's Garden. The San Jacinto Mountains have been uplifted more than 10,000 feet above Palm Springs by active geologic faults.

Facing page: A hot air balloon rises over the eastern valley. Several local companies that specialize in this unique mode of viewing the valley offer rides to the public.

These pages: The Empire Polo Club in Indio is part of the largest polo center in the United States. Matches generally are played from November through March.

Palm Springs is home to many familiar faces.
From left to right: Kirk Douglas is seen receiving a
Lifetime Achievement award at the 2005 Palm Springs
International Film Festival Gala, with author Sidney
Sheldon, and Jean Simmons, Douglas's co-star in
Spartacus looking on. Individual portraits are of
Nicole Kidman, Kevin Spacey, and Samuel Jackson.

Facing page: The ladies of the Fabulous Palm Springs Follies—who range in age from 60 to 84—regularly astound audiences with their artistically designed and intricately assembled costume creations.
PHOTO BY NED REDWAY, COURTESY OF THE FABULOUS PALM SPRINGS FOLLIES

Below, left: After careers on stage, in film and on television, the cast of the Follies has one goal remaining… to entertain audiences at every performance! This Long–Legged Lovely is old enough to collect Social Security.   PHOTO BY NED REDWAY, COURTESY OF THE FABULOUS PALM SPRINGS FOLLIES

Below, right: At age 84, Follies Lovely Dorothy Kloss holds the Guinness Record as "World's Oldest Still Performing Showgirl." PHOTO BY NED REDWAY, COURTESY OF THE FABULOUS PALM SPRINGS FOLLIES

These pages: Dune evening primroses thrive at the Coachella Valley Preserve. Their light color and pleasing fragrance attract night-flying insects, particularly moths that probe for nectar at the base of the floral tube. The prolific primrose produces many blossoms that may last only a day. It often grows in the company of pink-blossomed sand verbena.

Left: The San Jacinto Mountains catch snow that seldom reaches the lower elevations of Palm Springs.

Below: Palm Canyon holds precious pockets of water. The 15-mile–long canyon is a favored destination for hikers, who can see abundant vegetation such as desert fan palms, the only palm tree that is indigenous to California.

These pages: Colorful hot air balloons are particularly splendid at night, when owners light them up for the "balloon glow" during festivals.

Left and below: Joshua Tree National Park has twelve self-guided nature walks that take you into some of the most interesting sections of the park to see the geology and flora. The park encompasses 800,000 acres, with elevations ranging from just 900 feet above sea level to over 5,000 feet.

Some Joshua trees grow over 30 feet high. The trees, which are large yuccas, are a member of the lily family.

Right: The Living Desert, established in 1970, specializes in interpreting and conserving the plant and animal life of deserts around the world. This resident is a mountain lion, which has many common names such as puma, cougar, and panther.

Facing page: The African display at the reserve includes giraffes that are quite accustomed to curious people.

Below: Ostriches can sprint at speeds up to 50 miles per hour. They are native to dry, sandy parts of Africa.

These pages: Holiday lights brighten the station at the top of the Palm Springs Aerial Tramway. Winter tram riders who begin their ride in the mild weather at the valley station can rent snowshoes or cross-country skis at the top for a cool outdoor experience in Mount San Jacinto State Park.

Right: Joshua Tree National Park has more than 700 species of vascular plants. The wildflower season usually peaks between February and May.

Below: Lambs Creek spills down a rock face in the Oasis de Los Osos Reserve, north of Palm Springs. The reserve sits at the base of the Mount San Jacinto and protects numerous archaeological finds.

This page: The Moorten Botanical Gardens and Cactarium was started as an arboretum in 1938 by desert enthusiasts Patricia and Chester "Cactus Slim" Moorten. The complex harbors an extensive collection of cacti known for remarkable blooms. Clockwise from top left are the blooms of barrel cactus, prickly pear, and another prickly pear. The lower left is the blossom of a shrub, a desert bird of paradise, growing through a cactus.

Facing page: The Gardens shopping complex on El Paseo in Palm Desert invites browsers to its attractive lights and attractive landscaping.

These pages: The airy design of Palm Springs International Airport takes advantage of the balmy climate. At liftoff, spectacular views of the surrounding mountains can be seen. The concourse was named in honor of singer and entertainer Sonny Bono, who served as the area's congressman until his death in 1998.

Right and below: El Paseo has more than 300 shops, including boutiques, restaurants, and jewelers, along a 1-mile shopping section that boasts public art and extensive flower beds.

Far right: The Classic Club's Arnold Palmer–designed public golf course features 30 acres of lakes and streams.

Right: Date palms produce their sweet fruit for harvest, starting in September. The Coachella Valley is one of the nation's most important date-growing areas.

Below left and right: Vineyards in the Coachella Valley supply about 60,000 tons of table grapes annually. Per capita consumption of grapes in the United States is about eight pounds per year.

These pages: Camel safaris are a unique tourist attraction in the area. These visitors are trekking through the date groves in the Coachella Valley.

Above: Butterflies have good vision but a poor sense of smell. They are attracted to colorful flowers that bloom in dense clusters.

Left: More than 70,000 shorebirds have been counted at the Salton Sea during a single winter. It is an important site for migratory and wintering birds, such as these snow geese. In addition, the Salton Sea region is home to twenty-four species of reptiles and more than twenty species of mammals.

Above: Sunrise puts a remarkable glow on the rocky slopes of the San Jacinto Mountains. The range was uplifted by the immense pressure caused by the collision of the Pacific plate against the North American plate. The San Andreas Fault, at the foot of the mountains, is one of the better-known faults in North America.

Facing page: Strong fibers from the leaves of yuccas and agaves were traditionally used for weaving baskets. In Mexico, the agave was used to make tequila.

Right: An endangered bird, the least Bell's vireo, depends on the lush riparian vegetation along Chino Creek for nesting and raising its young. Chino Canyon also is home to endangered Peninsular bighorn sheep.

Below: Datura plants bloom in the shade of fractured rock in Andreas Canyon. The blossoms unfold in the evenings from a closed spiral to these beautiful open forms. A good hiking trail leads up the canyon, providing spectacular views of adjacent scenery and wildflowers.

Right: The El Mirador Hotel was a major tourist destination until it was converted to a hospital during World War II. Today it serves as the major medical center for Palm Springs, with the tower image used as the hospital's logo.

Far right: The Coachella Valley Bank on Palm Canyon Drive was designed by E. Stewart Williams in 1961. Today it houses Washington Mutual. Williams also designed the Palm Springs Art Museum and the mountain station of the Palm Springs Aerial Tramway.

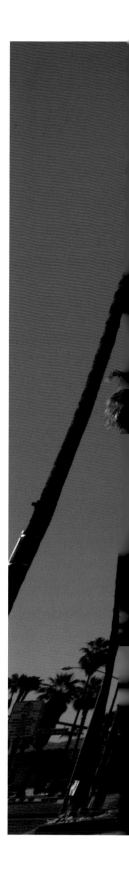

Left: The famous palm trees of Palm Springs soar into the last light of dusk. The city of Palm Springs contracts with landscapers to maintain the nearly 3,000 palm trees growing on city property.

Below: Elevations Restaurant at the top of the tram provides a stunning view over the Coachella Valley and surrounding mountains. The tramway is a historical civil engineering landmark. Construction began in 1961 and took two years. Engineers had to devise ingenious ways to surmount the steep natural terrain, including using helicopters to erect four of the five towers.

65

These pages: Horses provide a great way to get into the rugged mountains surrounding Palm Springs. Trails in the Indian Canyons Tribal Park take riders past the remnants of earlier settlements of the Agua Caliente Band of Cahuilla (pronounced Kaw-we-ah) Indians.

Above: Prince's plume was named for its resemblance to a showy feather in the cap of royalty. It grows only on soils that contain selenium, making it poisonous to livestock.

Right: Native fan palms thrive in Indian Canyons, above a field of brittlebush flowers in full bloom.

Left and below: The Children's Discovery Museum of the Desert, in Rancho Mirage, uses unique materials and the natural environment to inspire the natural curiosity of children.

Far left: The Palm Springs Art Museum contains an impressive permanent collection and hosts changing exhibitions as well as symposiums, performances, and classes.

These pages: Date palms each produce hundreds of individual dates on clusters. Between September and November the yellowish green fruits turn golden brown and are then harvested.

73

Right: The desert may be one of the finest places in the world to watch a sunrise.

Below: San Gorgonio Pass contains more than 4,000 windmills that provide enough electricity to power Palm Springs and the entire Coachella Valley.

Left: The fractured rocks, so representative of Joshua Tree National Park, are easily viewed at Jumbo Rocks, Split Rock, and Wonderland of Rocks.

Far left: A full moon hovers over the San Jacinto Mountains.

These pages: In downtown Palm Springs are bronze statues of famous residents, including Lucille Ball, who was one of the first Hollywood stars to "discover" the charms of Palm Springs, and Sonny Bono, who went into politics after ending his singing career with Cher.

Left: Unique public art on El Paseo enhances this attractive boulevard.

Below, left and right: Colorful outdoor sculptures are featured at the Palm Springs Art Museum. The museum was founded in 1938 to interpret the desert. It now is considered an oasis for modern and contemporary art.

Right: This giant century plant growing in Moorten Botanical Gardens is nicknamed Jaws.

Far right: Dubbed "the golf capital of the world," Palm Springs has more than one hundred golf courses, all offering splendid views of the surrounding peaks.

Below: Golden barrel cactus produces a circle of golden blossoms at the top, like a crown. These plants are just beginning to form buds.

These pages: Paragliders try to get aloft at the Salton Sea. This popular area is attractive to a variety of recreationists. Prominent activities include boating, birding, fishing, hiking, camping, and photography.

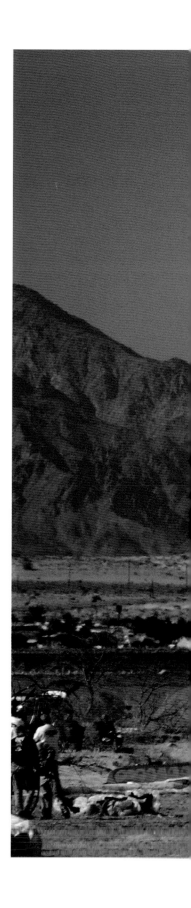

The annual multiday Coachella Music Festival showcases big-name entertainers and light shows every spring. The extravaganza brings in large crowds of revelers.

Facing page: The Tahquitz Canyon Visitor Center helps people learn about the area's tribal history, natural features, and wildlife.

Below, left: An ocotillo can have from six to as many as one hundred branches. Its unique silhouette is among the most recognizable in the Sonoran and Chihuahuan desert ecosystems.

Below, right: Desert Indian paintbrush often taps into the roots of larger, deep-rooted plants, so you'll see them growing in close proximity to shrubs.

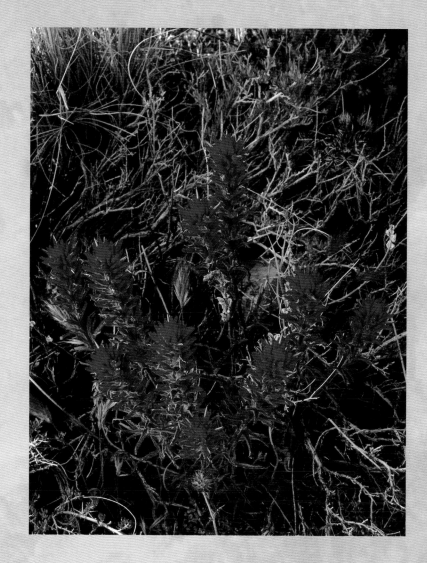

Above: Early-bird golfers are treated to the sunrise at the Desert Willow Golf Resort. The course was featured in *Smithsonian* magazine for its environmentally sound design and construction.

Facing page: The soft, intricate beauty of a cactus blossom belies the spiny barriers on the stems.

Left: The moon sets over the Coachella Valley Nature Preserve. The oasis, fringed by this unusual combination of sand dunes and palm trees, was formed when water seeped to the surface from a fault line near the San Andreas Fault.

Below: Called both sacred datura and jimsonweed, this plant has toxic and hallucinogenic qualities if ingested by humans.

Right: A member of the mustard family, Prince's plume grows through the Southwest.

Far right: Wind farms are erected in areas with average annual wind speeds of at least 13 miles per hour. In California, wind speeds are highest in hot weather; about three-fourths of the annual output is generated during the spring and summer.

Below: Beavertail cactus is commonly found between sea level and 4,000 feet. It blooms between April and June.

Left: In spring, the light is perfect just as the moon sets over Chino Canyon.

Below: This common plant, a crested cactus at Moorten Botanical Gardens, created a very unusual growth pattern.

These pages: The McCallum Adobe Museum houses the Palm Springs Historical Society. This was the first pioneer structure built in the area that is still standing. The owners also had the first telephone in Palm Springs. It is open for tours from mid-October through May.

These pages: The Palm Springs Historical Society on the Village Green maintains and displays Ruddy's General Store, a shop that operated in Palm Springs in the 1930s. The Society has also restored other structures that house memorabilia of earlier eras.

100

These pages: Functional can also be pleasingly artistic. The winter holidays inspire creative lighting, seen here at a wind farm and along the entrance to the Desert Regional Medical Center.

Joshua Tree National Park is crisscrossed by hundreds of faults. The San Andreas Fault extends along the south side of the park and the Blue Cut Fault runs through the park's center. The effects of faults and earthquakes are readily apparent throughout the area.

Right: Outdoor markets and street fairs are common in the mild climate, such as this one held at College of the Desert. Palm Springs boasts 354 days of sunshine a year. The price for that is less than 6 inches of rain annually.

Below: A horse–drawn carriage shares Palm Canyon Drive in downtown Palm Springs with snazzy convertibles and casual window shoppers.

Cimarrón Golf Resort's pond mirrors a perfect sunrise highlighting the summits of the San Jacinto Mountains.

The Palm Springs Aerial Tramway travels more than 2 miles from the valley floor into the mountains; the mountaintop averages thirty degrees cooler than the city.

Winter temperatures in Palm Springs average in the seventies, with nights in the mid-forties.

These pages: The Palm Springs Air Museum shelters one of the world's largest collections of flying World War II warplanes. The exhibits include airplanes, murals, uniforms, photographs, and video documentaries.

Right: Hikers take a break on the Murray Canyon Trail, which follows a palm-lined stream and ends at a series of small stone pools called Seven Sisters.

Below: Desert Canterbury bells find just enough shelter and moisture to live in the cracks between these rocks in Joshua Tree National Park.

Left: Edom Hill offers an outstanding vista of the wind turbines on San Gorgonio Pass.

Below: Detail of a palm frond.

A storm front moves over the mountains toward Palm Springs and is just about to let loose on the blooming desert sand verbena.

Palm Springs residents have imported dozens of species of palm trees from the Canary Islands, Japan, and Brazil, among others.